Thank you for reading my collection of poems and prose! Some pieces are personal and others are imaginative. Growing up, I have always loved creative writing and dreamt of one day publishing a collection. In this collection, I compiled some of my favorite pieces. The cover page is a print I made of a photograph of myself.

Contents

Sundays by the Seaside

A collection of poetry, prose, and art by Julie Xie

Until Dawn

This poem was inspired by the painting
Nighthawks by Edward Hopper

"Cup of coffee, please"

Stay with me tonight,
I can't keep my eyes off
that red dress.
It consumes me.

What a coincidence it is to meet
on the intersection of two streets;
let's hum the gentle serenade of the night,
together past midnight.

Like a picture in a frame,
we are on display,
for the world to see our
affairs in the dark.

We are *Nighthawks*,
trapped in the glass of our minds:
a microcosm of life
beyond our simple pursuits.

The usual bustle fades to
an eerie silence
when I am next to you.
Shhhhhh

"Pass the sugar, please"

Keep the sweetness to ourselves.
Perhaps it is a coincidence
that as the city is spinning,
we are right here.

I hope this coffee is strong enough
to keep me from drifting off,
so we can stay *Nighthawks*,
until dawn catches up.

Nightbird on the Watch

A thousand rivers between you and me
flowing from sea to sea.
Passing ships rumble round the dock,
I wait for one to stop.

But the ships keep rocking by,
so my heart wanders without solace or goodbye,
goodnight
I whisper, before letting the nightbird fly.

Nightbird cowers in the wind;
Mamabird told it to watch the riverbend.
To watch the tunnel of turbulent blues,
drift away without a ruse.

She said "don't be afraid,
the waters will subside someday."
Mamabird holds onto Nightbird
just enough to let her go.

"fly away," Mama calls from home,

"past the rivers and past the seas,
past the storms that break the breeze.
on the horizon, see the rising sun,
for a brief moment, the thousands will be just one."

A Late Winter

This winter was particularly less cool,
and I couldn't help but notice
what used to be
thick and full crumbled to defeat.

My giant winter coat, dry,
on the hanger. Didn't think about it until Spring,

until I packed it in a box labeled
"Winter" and thought
I may never need it again.

I remember years ago,
when the snow would swallow me whole.
I'd fit my tiny boots in the prints of Dad's
shoes. follow behind as he rolled up
a ball of snow.

This winter I returned
to the home of my recollection:

where the snow glistened like fireflies
and an air of nonchalance echoed
the moonlight.

But the chilly nights fade.
Dawn breaks early and dusk sleeps late.
The sunshine creeps in and the white
bleeds green.

A late winter,
came but never settled, passed like
a gentle whisper of air to the cheek,
a gentle blow of song to the ear.

This winter was particularly less cool,
and I can't help thinking
I may never see it again.

There's a Grand Life Ahead

My mother always told me
of a grand life ahead.

She envisioned a life of
glory. When I was a little girl,

I sat in the theaters next to her.
My small eyes

filled with fascination by what appeared
on the big screen:

Pictures of men and women dancing.
in top hats and feather dresses.

My mother always liked those old movies

Black and white, crowded ballrooms,
Ellington
in the back.

She envisioned a life of grandeur

like the ones in the movies. And I, too,
thought of one just like hers.

So, we climbed the stairs :together:
up and up in hopes of finding

a resemblance. And on our journey,
we passed fields of dreamers,

Swimming in oceans of red, white, and blue.
We watched colorful lights burst in the air

to the rhythm of a youthful nation.
The powder of freedom tickled our skin.

We kept climbing. At times the steps beneath our feet
crumbled.

But the film kept rolling. Black and white.
Men and women. Dancing.

Mother and I. held on for eighteen long years

Mother and I. can't climb any longer

the steps ahead are wearied down
by those infinitely strong.

perhaps we live in a dreamer's paradise,
where we are not suited to climb.

A Quintessential Sunday for the Bourgeoisie

This poem was inspired by the painting A Sunday
Afternoon on the Island of La Grande Jatte by Georges
Seurat

One by one, colorful sun shaders open.
The waters of the Seine are as still as the women's dresses:
heavy, it keeps them grounded.
The women sit in shade and indifference:
This beautiful Sunday
is like any other.

The men hold their walking sticks and wear top hats.
The women hold their children by their waist.
One girl
in a quaint flowing dress
runs and hollers.
Another examines her handful of flora.

The adults stilly sit, patiently waiting for
something, anything
to happen.
An air of arrogance
keeps them
still.
From bursting out in glee
or climbing the nearby trees.
Even the monkey
calmly remains in the shade:
unbothered by the world

Secluded yet not alone,
the women, men, children enjoy their leisurely time
surrounded by people of their own.

A Poem for Mama

I tell her that I can write,
and I can read. But she doesn't

believe me. I tell her that I can cook,
and I can clean. But she doesn't

believe me. And maybe my report cards
say otherwise. And maybe

my dumplings taste otherwise. But
Mama I have grown so much

since then. Remember that day
I drove the two of us

through pouring rain and freight
trains. *Mama you can trust me.*

If you can trust that the buds
will bloom in the Spring,

and the birds will sing songs
when morning calls,

and Daddy will come home
on that plane, then you can

trust me too.

A Poem for
Mama's Boy

I drink black coffee every
morning to wake me up

from six hours of sleepless
nights –Day in and day

out– Mama tells me
to study hard.

I sip my black coffee
lightly. That way I

don't lose any flavor. That way I
can taste the sourness. I swirl it

with my tongue.
It's disgusting.

I still drink it every
morning to wake me up

from six days in a week of
lonely work. I throw myself

into the abyss of lost hope
and I drown. It's confusing

like how poems are confusing.
like how first loves are confusing.

Only you are there to save me,
Mama's boy, from this endless

monotony. Every hour spent with you
is a shorter cup.

I play with my
Rubik's cube on my desk.

I don't know how to solve it.
And every time I touch it

the colors get more jumbled.
And I can see my frown

in the reflection of the shiny
square stickers.

As cynics come and go,
suppose this is my love poem.

To you and to her. Goodnight
Mama's Boy.

Sunday Night Blues

Stories for me to tell.

Shhhh. whisper it to me

Sunday nights no sleep,
sip of coffee in the basking light
that trickles through the open weave
curtains.

glorious is a feeling.
That languid morning, i pick myself up
to write a book.

Pen in hand, thoughts rewind,
stories , faint, but untold

I remember the gentle swaying of the trees,
rustle outside my window,
I remember the loud claps of thunder,
waking me from my sleep.

And mother would come in and tell me
stories, old, but untold.

My mother slept peacefully through the night
rain and thunder. She spoke soft words,
gentle dreams, for me to think of, And I slept
to the sounds of thunder,

My mind drifting off
to the sounds of thunder.

And i wouldn't wake till
Sunday morning.

Sunday nights no sleep,
I hold the pen and the ink bleeds
whirlwinds of mindless simmer.
unfiltered.

I wish i could write beautifully,
expressive thoughts,
Not stop.

I wish i could write stories
like the ones my mother told.

Sunday nights.
glorious as can be.
shhhh let your mind drift away

carried by the wave of your subconscious.
subdued, but unforgotten.

Beauty

I have always known that beauty lies in the soul;
it is something within, not without.
It is soft to touch, wispy, like cirrus clouds:
a bud that dances to a gentle lull.
It makes me feel simple among diamonds and gold.
Beauty is the seedling beginning to sprout:
the hibernating youth before the drought.
Or so I thought from the stories my momma told.
Little did I know nobody looks under the carpet,
for the things they are missing beg to be found.
That we wear blindfolds when going to the basement
and only hear blatant calls on the battleground.
Still, I hope that between cracks in cement
we see Beauty in the foundation: safe and sound.

We Keep Waiting

There's an ocean between us,
filled with exotic fish and algae.

Sometimes I dream of crossing a
bridge that stretches across the sea.

Sometimes I lay awake at night dreaming
of a wind that could whistle my songs,

and blow your scent, and scream at the currents
until they simmer down, and I stop holding on.

I have a hopeless dream that we could build a path
connecting my world to yours.

But there's an ocean between us,
that keeps closing unopened doors.

Perhaps even a million obstacles will never
stop my dream from following the currents.

Perhaps the world will finally stop raining
and that ocean will run dry.

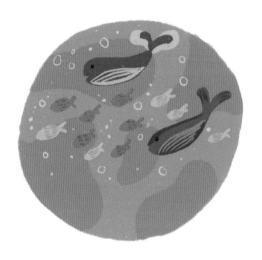

A Letter to a City

Three years since I last saw her:
bright face in the smiling sun.
Fragrance of sesame wind, meat bun shop
across the street –the neon sign–
shattered yet still strung across.

The street lamps beam
as her eyes blare in chaos. Her smile folds
in stripes, people cross
and cross.

She burns
when everyone's asleep.

For four years, I never saw her freckles shine,
lived beneath a canopy of shadow.

I waited
to see your light
to wish upon a star in the night.

Sometimes I try to hide it,
deny the presence in my body.
I'm not a city girl,
but you brought me into your big world.
You never listened to my heart beat, sweet and
salty.
Now I forget your embrace: a chilling warmth.

I never said your name right.
Shanghai

A Letter to a Town

Here, is the kind of place you hear green.

Here, summer breathes the children's cries
and diffuses it like a charge of ecstasy.
Here, the oak extends its lengthy arm
and brushes the hairs of passersby.

Here, we ride.
Pumping our legs, we take flight,
no mercy for anything in our way.
It's the Tour de Tricycle after all.

Flattened hair on shiny foreheads,
scuffed up knees from gravel streets,
The tour has come to an end,
we topple aside and bask in the light.

Here, we don't sleep.
Half awake in conscious oblivion
living a merry-go-round
of raw joy.

Here, is close to heart,
yet too far to call home.
like a lost signal
my memory fades.

Trees are trees
but now and again
the laughter echoes
till I hear green.

Je Suis à un Appel

Tu cours dans mes bras
tu fuis le monde
quand il y a une petite frayeur
quand il y a un peu de danger.

Mes bras sont toujours ouverts,
si le monde es injuste
si le monde s'en moque
si le monde vous ignore.

Mes bras sont toujours ouverts,
quand tu te sens comme un étranger
quand tu te sens incompris.
Je suis à un appel.

Parce que je te comprendrai toujours
meme quand tu te sens seul,
tu n'es jamais vraiment seul.
Je suis à un appel, mon ami.

Dumpling Days

1. prepare the dough

"My little girl. So naive." My dad smiles while kneading the dumpling dough in circular motions.

I watch his arms rotate in meticulous motions, pounding each blob of dough into little tortillas. I watch him stuff the dumpling with his own mixture of ground beef, tofu, and veggies, and then pinch the edges together to create a crescent moon shape. My mind traced dad's dumpling procedure until several arrays of dumplings were ready to be steamed.

When the dumplings were cooked and plated, everyone dived in except for me. I despised the taste of dumplings. In my opinion, they were always too soggy, too oily, or too many veggies. One day, as any blunt little girl would do, I told my dad.

He looked at me with slight disappointment and replied, "You may hate them now, but when you grow up and there's nobody there to make dumplings for you, what're you going to do."

I looked at him blankly. "Nah, I just don't like dumplings."

"No, no, you will like them one day, but by then, you won't be able to get them. You will miss it."

"ok."

2. stuff the dough

I watched dad make dumplings the weekends he doesn't have work.
The process so vivid, it is permanently ingrained into my brain.
When I got old enough, I copied dad's procedure. I stuffed them like
he did. I folded them like he did. For a while, there was no visible
difference in mine compared to his. But quickly after I mastered the
basic steps, I could not be restrained by the monotonous homogeny
of each dumpling. As always, I let my artistic eye guide the way; I
made square-shaped, people-shaped, and a whole collection of
amorphous blobs. Although I avoided eating dumplings, these
somehow tasted a lot better.

Years later, I linger around Chinatown in Massachusetts. I see a
dumpling stall. I go in and browse the available options. I browse for
quite a long time until I realize I don't want dumplings. I wasn't even
sure why I was in there. But in my mind I imagine my dad cheerfully
asking the clerk for all the flavors:

"Yes, the shrimp, the vegetable..." He looks down at me and asks,
"What do you like Julie?"

"Ummm, I like the shrimp but that's it."

"Ok, let's bring these dumplings home, cook some for your brother
and mom. Do you think they'll like that?"

"ok!"

My dad holds my hand, and we walk out of the store. He drove, and I called shotgun. Luminous hues of orange and pink pervade the horizon. Our weekly dumpling errand was nothing out of the ordinary, yet special to say the least.

3. pinch and fold edges together

I sighed and left the store empty-handed.

My dad was wrong; I don't miss dumplings.

I miss the thought of him making it. I miss being there on Saturday mornings, watching his arms knead the dough into flat pancakes, his face full of glee as we present our creations to the rest of the family. The farther I walk from home, the taller I get, the heavier my backpack becomes, I miss it even more: our special routine. It was unique to just us. Entrapped in silent observations, now and then a chuckle, we formed an unbreakable bond. Eyes wide open, I followed his motions until they were seared into my brain. He knew I was watching, for now, and then, he slowed down so I could get a good view of how to pinch the edges like the rocking ocean waves.

My footsteps reflect my usual midday blues. I glance at some of the other stores around: milk tea, salon, dim sum. Apart from the occasional chattering, the streets were clear. Chinatown sure isn't China if it's this quiet, I thought. The China I knew was flashy signs, voices shrouded in voices, grand hotels, and even grander shopping plazas.

Sometimes I miss the commotion. Chopsticks swerving left and right, plates colliding against each other, laughter echoing through every word: this is dumplings at family reunions. They were filled with flattery, affectations, and excessive courtesy: the opposite of dumplings at home. Home was tranquil and comforting. Words of love were not spoken; they were implied. Quiet and peace suit me much better, I decide.

4. steam dumplings

My home was not dumplings. Nor was it flashy signs and grand hotels. It was family dinners and late night television, brick house with a driveway, and the weekend fresh produce market. The air outside was so quiet, I could hear the ocean waves.

It is a beautiful day, a rarity in Shanghai. Dad is cooking. Mom is reading her updates on last night's basketball game. William is moping around, probably looking for me.

Only I'm not there.

I'm here, on the other side of the world, writing about dumplings.

5. start a new plate

A fresh plate of dumplings sits before me. I made them myself, but I used dad's recipe. I take a bite of one; the steamy flavor burns my tongue. The taste reminds me of those dumpling days.

It's a beautiful day in Massachusetts. With Charles River flowing on my left and lines of brick condos on my right, I drove into the afternoon sun. Even though there was a hopeless road ahead, devoid of dumpling days, I pressed my foot against the gas pedal, leaving the dumpling routine behind me. For there is something much better ahead: a future filled with my own creations and people to share them with.

Life is too short to dwell on the past.

31

About the Author

Julie Xie was born in Rhode Island. Besides going to school, she likes to play tennis and basketball with her brother. She spent her childhood in North Carolina and teenage years in Shanghai. She currently lives in suburban Massachusetts with her family.